MIGHTY ALEX

WRITTEN BY

INGRID ULLRICH

ILLUSTRATED BY

ELEONORA CALI

MIGHTY ALEX

Written by Ingrid Ullrich

For My Nephew, Alex

May you always forge your own path while shining
bright, like the shooting star that you are.

This book belongs to

Once there was a little boy named Alex,
Full of energy, he had many special talents.

Loud and proud, he would never sit still,
Unless building blocks, then he'd do it at will.

Quick to learn, never missing a beat,
Always the first with his homework complete.

Clever he was and so very wise,
But there were some things Alex needed to realize...

When Mommy and Daddy said the word "No,"
This wasn't a debate but the final say so.

ABCDEF
GHILMN
OPQRST
UVWZ
2+2=
123456
789 10 11
12 14 15 16
17 18 19 20

Or when the teacher says, "Please sit down,"
It's hard to teach with kids running around.

How would it feel if a friend did this to you,
When trying to teach them something new?

BISCUITS
BOOK OF RULES

Life can seem tough with so many rules,
But they are important as our learning tools.

LET'S
PLAY
PS5
HIPS

They teach us how to get along with others,
Like taking turns in video games with your brother.

WHERE DO WE GO?

As you get older, rules will help you throughout,
When trying to decide on, "What's the best route?"

ALEX
CEO

A natural leader, so bold, bright, and strong,
Alex knew in his heart what to do all along.

And so, the next day he went to his class,
"Good Morning," he said, to each person he passed.

The teacher then noticed for several days,
How Alex was helpful in so many ways.

He jumped off the bus and rushed through the door,
"Look, Mommy and Daddy, what this medal is for!"

Before they could answer, Alex shouted with glee,
"Best helper and making others feel happy!"

Then Mommy and Daddy, with tears in their eyes,
Looked at each other and started to cry.

"Actually, I am going to give this to you.
You were the ones who taught me what to do."

"I don't need an award to make me act kind,
I do it for how it makes me feel inside."

The End!